Noah's Ark
and Other Bible Favorites

ARCTURUS

The Creation

> *Genesis 1:26 Then God said, "And now we will make human beings; they will be like us and resemble us. They will have power over the fish, the birds, and all the animals, domestic and wild, large and small."*

In the beginning, the world was covered in water and everything was dark. The Spirit of God moved over the water.

One day, God said, "Let there be light!" and the Earth was filled with light. God was pleased with this and called the light "day" and the darkness "night." Evening passed of the very first day, then morning came.

On the second day, God said, "Let there be a space above the oceans, to separate the heavens from the earth." God named this space "sky."

On the third day, God said, "Let dry ground appear from the waters." He named the dry ground "land," and the waters "seas." Then God commanded, "Let the land produce plants and crops and fruit trees of every kind." The land filled with beautiful trees and plants.

On the fourth day, God commanded, "Let lights appear in the sky to separate day from night, to mark the days, the seasons, and the passing of the years." God named the two great lights the "sun," to rule over the day, and the "moon," to rule over the night, separating light from darkness.

On the fifth day, God said, "Let the waters be filled with all kinds of living creatures, and let the air be filled with birds." God blessed the creatures and told them to make the skies and water their new homes.

The next day, God said, "Let the earth produce many kinds of animal life, tame and wild, large and small." And He was pleased with what He saw.

On the sixth day, God said, "Now I shall make human beings in my image. They will rule the earth and the other creatures." God created a man in His image and called him Adam. Blessing him, God said, "Look after everything I have created. I have provided you with everything you could ever need."

By the seventh day, God had finished His creation and He needed to rest. He blessed the seventh day, because it was His special day of rest.

Eve's Temptation

Genesis 3:6 The woman saw how beautiful the tree was and how good its fruit would be to eat, and she thought how wonderful it would be to become wise.

God planted a beautiful garden, called Eden, for Adam to live in. It was filled with animals, plants, flowers, and trees bearing delicious fruit. There were also two special trees, the tree of life and the tree of the knowledge of good and evil.

"You may eat the fruit from every tree in the garden, except the tree of the knowledge of good and evil," said God, "for if you do, you will die."

Adam was happy in the Garden of Eden, but he was lonely. Seeing this, God took out one of Adam's ribs while he was asleep and created a woman from it, called Eve. She became Adam's wife and they lived happily in the garden until, one day, they met a cunning snake.

"Did God really tell you not to eat from the tree of the knowledge of good and evil?" asked the snake.

"Yes," said Eve. "If we even touch the fruit from the tree, we will die."

"Oh, that isn't true," hissed the snake. "God only told you that because He knows that when you eat from that tree you will become like Him. You will know what is good and what is evil."

The devious snake wound its way up the tree. Eve looked up and, unable to resist, she picked the enticing fruit and began to eat it. Then, as the snake wriggled away, Eve offered some to Adam.

Suddenly, everything in Eden seemed different. The fruit had given Adam and Eve understanding. Realizing they were naked, they covered their bodies with fig leaves.

"Why did you eat the fruit from the forbidden tree?" asked God.

"Eve gave me the fruit," replied Adam, bowing his head in shame.

"It was the snake's fault. He told me that if I ate the fruit I would become as wise as you," said Eve.

Filled with anger, God punished Adam and Eve. "Through your disobedience, pain and suffering have come into the world," He told them. "From now on, your lives will be marked by hardship." With that, He banished them from the Garden of Eden for ever.

Did you know?

In Hebrew, the name Adam means "mankind."

Cain and Abel

Genesis 4:7 *"If you had done the right thing, you would be smiling; but because you have done evil, sin is crouching at your door. It wants to rule you, but you must overcome it."*

After they had disobeyed God, life became hard for Adam and Eve. But they found happiness in their two sons, Cain and Abel.

Abel grew up to be a shepherd, tending his flocks in the hills and watching over them in all weathers. Cain was a farmer, going out into the fields every day to dig the earth ready for planting seeds.

One day, Cain chose some of his crops—a few vegetables and some fruit—to give as an offering to God. They were not the best crops he had grown, but Cain thought they were good enough.

Abel was more thoughtful, and believed that everything he had belonged to God, so he

offered the Lord the finest sheep from his flock.

God was pleased with Abel's gift, but He rejected Cain's offering. Cain was furious, and shouted at his younger brother.

God told Cain, "If you had given freely to me, like your brother, then you would have won my approval, too. Instead, you resented giving me even the smallest amount of food."

Cain then asked Abel to walk with him in the fields and, when they were alone, Cain killed his brother.

"Cain, where is your brother, Abel?" asked God.

"I have no idea," said Cain. "Am I my brother's keeper?"

But God had seen what Cain had done. "Why have you done this terrible thing?" He asked. "I can clearly see your brother's blood on your hands! For your terrible sins, you must leave this land to wander the earth aimlessly for ever."

"But God, whoever meets me will know you have punished me and will want to kill me themselves."

But God told Cain, "I will protect you. If anyone kills you, seven lives will be taken in revenge."

With that, God put a mark on Cain to warn people not to kill him, then sent him to the land of Nod to wander the earth for ever.

Noah's Ark

Genesis 7:1 The Lord said to Noah, "Go into the boat with your whole family; I have found that you are the only one in all the world who does what is right."

As the centuries passed, God became disappointed with the bad lives people had chosen to live. But there was one man who pleased Him. His name was Noah.

"I am very disappointed in the people I have created, so have decided to punish them by flooding the world," God told Noah. "But because you have lived such a good life, I shall save you and your family."

God told Noah to build an ark that would be big enough for him and his wife, their three sons and their wives, and two of every kind of animal and bird. Just as Noah had finished building the ark, it began to rain, so Noah filled the ark with hundreds of creatures.

For many days the rain fell. Rivers overflowed, and everything outside the ark perished. After a hundred and fifty days, the water level began to drop and the ark came to rest on the tip of Mount Ararat.

Noah wanted to know if the earth was dry enough for everyone to leave the boat, so he released one of the ravens from the ark to see if it could find land. But the raven did not return. Noah then released a dove, but it returned with no news.

After another seven days, Noah released the dove again. This time it returned the same evening, carrying an olive leaf in its beak. It had found dry land!

The Rainbow Promise

Genesis 8:21 "Never again will I put the earth under a curse because of what people do; I know that from the time they are young their thoughts are evil," said the Lord.

When Noah, his family and all the animals and birds were safely on dry land, God looked down upon them and made a promise.

"Now you are back on land, you are free to find new homes for your families. Release the animals so they, too, can find new homes and the world can become full again," said God. "But I promise that no matter how wickedly people decide to live their lives, never again will I send a flood to destroy the earth. If it rains for a long time and you fear I have forgotten this promise, look up at the sky and I will show you a sign that I have not forgotten."

As Noah and his family looked up, a beautiful rainbow arched across the sky.

"The rainbow will always remind you of my promise to every creature that roams this land, for now and all of time," God said to them.

In the years that followed, Noah, who lived to be very old, often looked up at the beautiful rainbows in the sky and remembered God's promise. He served God faithfully every day of his long and happy life.

The Tower of Babel

Genesis 11:4 They said, "Now let's build a city with a tower that reaches the sky, so that we can make a name for ourselves and not be scattered all over the earth."

After the great flood, Noah's descendants spread over the earth in various directions. One group decided they would like to make their home in Babylonia, and began to learn how to make bricks and to build houses.

Then it was suggested they build a huge, magnificent city: "We can even make the tallest tower in the world and then we'll be the best!"

God watched as work began on the tower. He saw the walls getting higher and people's ideas getting bigger. He knew they would soon believe anything was possible—these people were starting to think they were gods among men!

So, before the tower was finished, God decided to punish them for their vanity by confusing their language. Instead of speaking the same language, they would all now speak different languages.

There was chaos! The builders could not understand a word they were saying to each other, and the people could no longer make their great plans.

The great tower was left unfinished, and became known as the Tower of Confusion, or the Tower of Babel.

The Birth of Isaac

Genesis 21:8 The child grew, and on the day that he was weaned, Abraham gave a great feast.

When Abraham was ninety-nine years old, God visited him and told him that his wife, Sarah, would soon give him a son. Abraham was very surprised to hear this and wondered if a man could have a child when he was so old!

"Can Sarah give birth to a child even though she is ninety years old?" Abraham asked God. "Why not just let Ishmael, my son by Hagar, be my heir?"

"No, your wife Sarah will bear you a son and you will name him Isaac," said the Lord, who had other plans for Ishmael.

When Sarah learned she was to bear Abraham a son, she was shocked and found it very hard to believe. But the Lord kept his promise, and exactly nine months later, when Abraham was a hundred years old, Sarah gave birth to a baby boy.

Abraham named the child Isaac, just as God had told him to do.

"After so many years of longing for a child of my own, God has brought me joy and laughter," said Sarah. "Everyone who hears about the birth of Isaac will be overjoyed and wish us great happiness."

Abraham's Test

Genesis 22:15 "I promise that I will give you as many descendants as there are stars in the sky or grains of sand along the seashore. Your descendants will conquer their enemies."

Isaac grew up to be a wonderful son to Abraham and Sarah. God saw that they were very happy and decided to test Abraham's faith.

One day, God told Abraham, "Take your son, Isaac, to the land of Moriah. When you get there, you must offer him as a sacrifice to me."

Sadness and rage filled Abraham's heart. How could the Lord ask him to kill the son he loved so much? But Abraham knew he had to do as God commanded, and set off for Moriah with Isaac and two servants.

After three days, Abraham saw Moriah in the distance. "Stay here," he commanded the servants, "while Isaac and I go and pray."

Abraham made an altar of bricks and tied Isaac on it. With tears in his eyes, he raised his knife to kill the son he loved.

Suddenly, the angel of the Lord called to him, "Do not hurt him! The Lord sees that you honor and obey him, because you were prepared to offer your son to him despite your sadness."

For his obedience, God showered Abraham with blessings and said he would have as many descendants as there were stars in the sky.

Jacob and Esau

*Genesis 27:24 And he said, "Are you really my son Esau?"
And he said, "I am."*

Jacob and Esau were twin boys born to Isaac and his wife Rebekah. God said that Jacob would one day be the head of the family, even though Esau was the elder.

Isaac favored his elder son, Esau, who was a skilled hunter, but Rebekah preferred Jacob, who was quiet and thoughtful.

When Isaac was very old and going blind, he told Esau to go hunting. "When you have made me a tasty stew with the meat, I will give you my final blessing before I die," he said weakly.

Rebekah was determined that Jacob would receive the blessing to rule the family instead of Esau. So, when Esau had left the house, she told Jacob to fetch two goats from the field, which she used to make a stew. She then told Jacob to dress in some of Esau's clothes, so Isaac would not recognize him, and to put the goatskins on his arms to make them like Esau's hairy arms.

"Which son are you?" asked Isaac, when Jacob gave him the stew.

"I am Esau," said Jacob, leaning over to kiss his father.

Isaac could smell Esau's clothes and feel his hairy arms, so he gave the younger son his blessing. Jacob was now to be head of the family after Isaac's death.

Jacob's Ladder

Genesis 28:20-21 Then Jacob made a vow to the Lord. "If you are with me and protect me on the journey I am making and give me food and clothing, and if I return safely to my father's home, then you will be my God."

When Esau learned that Jacob had tricked his father, he was extremely angry. Rebekah then sent Jacob away to live with her brother, Laban, in Haran.

On his journey, Jacob stopped to rest. He fell asleep and dreamed he saw a stairway reaching from earth to Heaven, with angels traveling up and down it. At the very top of the stairway there was a brilliant light, and a voice said, "I am the Lord, the God of Abraham and Isaac. I will give you and all of your descendants all this land that you are resting on and the land all around it. Through you and your many descendants I will bless all the nations. Wherever you go, I will protect you and bring you back to this land. I will never leave you until I have done all that I have promised you."

"The Lord is here and he is with me!" thought Jacob, when he woke the next morning.

Taking the stone he had used to rest his head, Jacob set it up as a memorial to God. Although he felt a little afraid, Jacob was also happy. "I have found the house of God!" he said. "This must be the gate that opens into Heaven."

The Coat of Many Colors

Genesis 37:3 Jacob loved Joseph more than all his other sons, because he had been born to him when he was old.

Jacob went on to marry and had twelve sons. His favorite son was Joseph, his youngest.

Jacob gave Joseph a special many-colored coat, which Joseph's brothers felt should have been given to the firstborn son. This made the other brothers jealous.

The brothers hated Joseph even more when he told them about his dreams, in which he had seen his brothers and his father all bowing down to him.

"Huh! So you think you are going to be a king and rule over us, do you?" they sneered. Even Jacob was angry when he heard about the dreams.

When Joseph went out to check his flocks one day, his brothers kidnapped him, and sold him to some merchants who were passing by. The brothers then stained Joseph's special coat with animal blood, and showed it to Jacob. "Some wild animals captured Joseph and ripped him to pieces in the field," they said.

Poor Jacob was inconsolable. "Now I will live in sorrow until the day I die," he sobbed.

Joseph in Egypt

Genesis 39:6 Potiphar handed over everything he had to the care of Joseph, and did not concern himself with anything, except the food he ate.

Joseph was sold as a slave to Potiphar, an officer of the king of Egypt. With God watching over him, Joseph worked hard and succeeded in everything he did, which soon drew his master's attention.

Realizing that his new slave was different to all his other servants, Potiphar put Joseph in charge of his household and all his business.

Potiphar spent all his time eating, drinking, and having a good time, while Joseph took care of everything.

Joseph was handsome, and Potiphar's wife fell in love with him.

But Joseph was loyal to Potiphar, who had treated him well, so when his master's wife made advances toward him, Joseph rejected her.

To be turned away by a servant was a great insult, so Potiphar's wife lied, and told the other servants that Joseph had tried to attack her. "Look, he ran away, leaving his coat behind!" she screamed.

Even Potiphar believed his wife's lies, and had Joseph arrested and thrown in prison. But even there, God was with Joseph, and helped him every day.

ARCTURUS

This edition published in 2012 by Arcturus Publishing Limited
26/27 Bickels Yard, 151–153 Bermondsey Street,
London SE1 3HA

ISBN: 978-1-84858-676-5
CH002338US
Supplier 15, Date 0412, Print run 1750

Printed in China